I0884353

Consultants

Timothy Rasinski, Ph.D.
Kent State University

Lori Oczkus, M.A.
Literacy Consultant

Christopher Nyerges
Author and Educator;
Cofounder of School of Self-Reliance

Publishing Credits

Rachelle Cracchiolo, M.S.Ed., *Publisher*
Conni Medina, M.A.Ed., *Managing Editor*
Dona Herweck Rice, *Series Developer*
Emily R. Smith, M.A.Ed., *Content Director*
Stephanie Bernard and Seth Rogers, *Editors*
Robin Erickson, *Multimedia Designer*

The TIME logo is a registered trademark of TIME Inc. Used under license.

Image Credits: p.19 Bruno Boissonnet/Science Source; p.26 The Print Collector/Alamy; p.31 Sabena Jane Blackbird/Alamy; p.39 illustration by Kevin Pham; All other images from iStock and/or Shutterstock.

Notes: Care and caution should always be practiced when using tools and methods for survival. The answers to the mathematics problems posed throughout the book are provided on page 48.

Library of Congress Cataloging-in-Publication Data

Names: Rice, William B. (William Benjamin), 1961- author.
Title: Struggle for survival. Shelter / William B. Rice.
Other titles: Shelter
Description: Huntington Beach, CA : Teacher Created Materials, [2016] | Audience: Grades 4 to 6. | Includes bibliographical references and index.
Identifiers: LCCN 2016016966 (print) | LCCN 2016017503 (ebook) | ISBN 9781493836048 (pbk.) | ISBN 9781480757080 (eBook)
Subjects: LCSH: Survival--Juvenile literature.
Classification: LCC GF86 .R5255 2016 (print) | LCC GF86 (ebook) | DDC 613.6/9--dc23
LC record available at https://lccn.loc.gov/2016016966

Teacher Created Materials
5301 Oceanus Drive
Huntington Beach, CA 92649-1030
http://www.tcmpub.com

ISBN 978-1-4938-3604-8

© 2017 Teacher Created Materials, Inc.

Printed by: 51497
Printed in: China

How Did I Get Here?

It happens. Not to everyone and not every day, but it *does* happen. Somewhere, someone is struggling with a survival situation. Maybe the day started out as usual and then something went wrong. Maybe the person got lost on an isolated highway, or maybe an unforeseen **natural disaster** took the person by surprise. You never know.

And that's really the point: *you never know*. So what can we do in a world where anything can happen? Are we simply victims of random negative experiences? Is the world shouting to us, "Hey, good luck with that."?

Doomsday Possibilities

Many people have gone to great lengths to prepare for worldwide doomsday events. These might include nuclear wars or large meteors striking Earth. And sure, these are *possibilities*. But it is best to consider the *probabilities*. The truth is that these events are very, very unlikely.

Table of Contents

Survival: What Is It?

Survival is a popular topic today. It seems to be everywhere. It is on the Internet, in bookstores, and even on television. But when we investigate the word *survival* (which basically means “to keep living”), we might think, “Hey, I’m surviving right now!” In a sense, that’s true. But the survival we’re talking about is really more than that. It’s nitty-gritty. It’s intense surviving through the most extreme and challenging conditions, such as natural disasters or situations such as getting lost on a hike or having car trouble far from any city or town. What would *you* do if something like that happened to you?

We have become comfortable these days in our **industrialized** world. We have heaters and air conditioners. We have ready-made houses with indoor plumbing. And our clothes can be bought from a store. But humans have lived for hundreds of thousands of years without these **creature comforts**. Dealing with extreme heat, extreme cold, or being wet to the bone can be physically difficult. Even more, the emotional and mental challenges can outweigh the physical issues.

No! Sure, emergency and even **catastrophic** events and circumstances can happen, but the answer to them isn't being lucky. The answer is to be prepared. There are many ways to prepare for such emergency situations. And, even though it is unlikely they will happen to you, if something *does* happen, you don't need to worry or panic. You can be confident because you are smart and you are prepared.

Yes, bad things happen, but the most important thing to remember is that human beings have tools, **resources**, and the brainpower to deal with them, to manage them, and to survive them.

THINK LINK

- Have you or anyone you know been in a survival situation?
- What emergency plans do you and your family have in place?
- What emergency plans does your city or town have in case of disaster?

Extreme Temperatures!

In Death Valley, California, the average high temperature in July is 116°F (46°C). The average low temperature in January is 38°F (3°C). What is the difference between the two temperatures in degrees Fahrenheit?

Three Priorities

In developing a response to an emergency situation, you should always consider three key **priorities**:

- Secure your personal safety.
- Maintain your body temperature.
- Maintain your body's **hydration**.

The Most Important Things to Remember

> ***"Do what you can with what you have, where you are."***
>
> **—Theodore Roosevelt**

Most people prefer comfort to challenges. But challenges may come to your door whether you want them or not! To manage and live through them, it's good to have some ideas of what to do when they occur. This gives you confidence—and it makes you **competent** to survive. It may also help to remember that many people in the world today live without the creature comforts you may take for granted. It's possible to live (and live well) without them.

There are many survival experts in the world who have experimented with different survival methods. But, for living through challenging situations, most experts recognize three key factors. They are preparation, **composure**, and strategy.

So what does any of this have to do with shelter? When it comes to survival, **exposure** is often a top concern. Sometimes it's *the* top concern. When exposure in a harsh environment is a possibility, it's best to be prepared. And if you are not prepared, be sure to maintain your composure. This will help you develop a successful strategy.

Know It!

There are many useful **survival skills**. Some of the most useful are fire making, plant identification, shelter building, **orienteering**, and **navigation**.

Deadly Weather

In recent years, 5,219 people died in the United States from temperature-related causes. Cold caused 3,192 deaths. Heat caused 2,027 deaths.

The Bare Facts: Preparation, Composure, and Strategy

Preparation gives you the best overall chance to survive. But how do you prepare when it comes to shelter, including clothing (the first layer of shelter your body has)? You prepare by knowing where you are going, what you will be doing, and the potential for exposure. You also do this by keeping emergency supplies on hand that will help provide the warmth—or protection from heat—that you need.

In reality, you do this every day. When you dress for the day, you prepare for the **elements**. If it looks like rain, you might bring a raincoat. If it's very hot, you'll mainly stay indoors or in shaded areas.

Preparing for survival means taking your daily practice a step further. Rather than simply planning for possibilities in a single day, you think ahead. You plan and also keep emergency supplies on hand. You never know what might happen and what extra protection you may need. Being prepared may keep a surprising situation from becoming a survival situation.

THINK LINK

- How do you protect yourself from the elements every day?
- How often do you find yourself too cold, too hot, or wearing clothes that don't allow you to do what you want or need to do?
- In what ways should you better prepare yourself when it comes to the clothes you wear?

Supply List

Many experts suggest that emergency supplies should be kept for each person and pet in a home. You should make sure there are enough supplies to last about three days. Supplies should include things for essential needs such as water, food, shelter, light, communication, first aid, and **sanitation**.

Composure

Above all, when an emergency situation or event occurs, it is very important to maintain your composure. Keep calm, and don't let fear and emotion take over. In this way, you can think clearly about your situation and figure out what to do. If you begin to get anxious or focus on fear, there's a simple first step: stop and breathe. Sit and take several deep breaths until you relax. When you get excited and fearful, the parts of your brain responsible for reasoning begin to close down. This makes it difficult to think clearly.

Strategy

The brain is a powerful tool, so use it! One great strategy for handling challenging situations is known as the OODA Loop. The OODA Loop is short for **O**bserve, **O**rient, **D**ecide, and **A**ct. *Observe* so you know what you are facing. *Orient* yourself to determine your location and your place in it. *Decide* on an action or series of actions. *Act* on your decision and commit to it.

But remember, OODA is meant to be a loop or a cycle. You must *keep observing* and *keep orienting* so that you are ready to take advantage of new opportunities. Be ready to make a new decision or take a different action, if necessary.

And remember this as well: keep checking your attitude, your emotions, and your physical condition. Stay positive! In a survival situation, that can make all the difference.

Persistence, Not Perfection

Remember, sometimes we can do everything right, make no mistakes, and still fail. Other times, we might make several mistakes and still succeed. So, go easy on yourself. Don't expect perfection, and don't be a quitter. Break things down into small, simple tasks, and keep completing each task one at a time.

The Best for Everyone

You and three friends are stranded in a warm, sunny climate. You have a 10-foot square of fabric you can use for additional protection. What is the best way to use it to maximize its benefits: one big square or cut into pieces?

Exposure and Body Temperature

When people die in the wilderness, it is easy to believe that they must have died from hunger or thirst. But actually, there is a factor that is more likely to result in death in wilderness survival situations. It is exposure to the elements. That is, people freeze to death or die from overheating.

Sweet Spot

There are certain air temperatures that are easier on our bodies than others. The best range for humans to maintain body temperature without stress is 79°F to 86°F (26°C to 30°C).

Rule of 3

There is a popular general rule that many people use in survival situations. It states that a person can survive . . .

- 3 minutes without air
- 3 hours without shelter
- 3 days without water
- 3 weeks without food

Of course, people have been known to survive longer than these restrictions. But the rule helps as a general guide.

So, paying attention to your body and your surroundings must be a top priority. You've got to make sure that you stay warm in cold weather and keep cool in hot weather. In everyday life, you know what to do in extreme heat or extreme cold. Both conditions usually mean it's best to stay indoors. You might even see a warning on television. Extreme heat calls for limited activity, plenty of shade, lots of liquids, and air conditioning—if you have it. Extreme cold calls for bundling up and having a heat source such as a heater or a fireplace. But in a survival situation in the wilderness, things are very different. We must adapt to our surroundings.

Human beings are highly adaptable. We are able to live in many different environments in many different places on Earth. A key factor that enables us to do this is our ability to make things to help us survive in different places. We make clothes; we make shelters such as houses, huts, and tents; and we also make fire. All of these things help us maintain our body temperatures.

Losing Heat

There are several different ways we can lose heat from our bodies. The more you know about the different ways, the more you can protect against them. *Conduction* is the loss of heat through direct contact with a colder object, such as the cold ground. *Convection* is the loss of heat through air currents, such as the wind. *Radiation* is the loss of heat through basic energy release. *Evaporation* is the loss of heat when water carries away energy by changing to a gas (water vapor through sweating). *Respiration* is the loss of heat and water vapor by breathing.

The Elements

Innovative technology has allowed inventors to create products to minimize the effects of nature's elements. Elements are factors in nature. These include hot and cold air, rain and snow, and flooding and wind. When they reach extreme conditions, they can threaten life. But remember that nature is not our enemy. Earth and its atmosphere are doing what they have always done.

While rain and snow might make us uncomfortable, they also provide us with the water we need. Heat, cold, and wind can be harsh, and flooding can be dangerous for us. But these are some of the ways that the atmosphere maintains its energy balance. The plants and animals around the world depend on the changes these conditions bring to keep living through their cycles of life.

Love for Mother Nature

We shouldn't think of nature as an opponent to be conquered. Rather, we need to remember that our bodies and brains have enabled our species to survive in nature for hundreds of thousands of years. We just have to use our own resources wisely.

Flash Flood!

Flash floods can happen when a lot of rain falls in a short amount of time. The water doesn't have time to drain as it normally would. It doesn't take much water to cause damage, either. Just 6 inches of fast-moving floodwater can knock over an adult. Only 2 feet of floodwater is strong enough to move a bus. If the water level rises 7.5 inches per hour, how long would it take to reach 2 feet of water?

Paying attention to your body and the elements may be the most important part of survival. This includes noticing the outside temperature and how our bodies respond to it. Forgetting nature's balance and not attending to the elements can lead to problems. We can find ourselves in tough situations. And if we're not careful, those situations can have **dire** consequences.

Hypothermia

Hypothermia means "under heated." It is the condition in which a person's body doesn't maintain a healthy temperature. This happens when a person is exposed to cold air and does not have enough protection to stay warm. Protection includes clothes and shelter. It also includes a heat source, such as fire. If a person has hypothermia, getting warm should be the first priority. Otherwise, freezing to death is a strong possibility.

Normal Human Temperature Range

Most people know that the normal average body temperature is 98.6°F (37°C). However, your temperature can vary throughout the day. In the mornings, it might be just below average at 98°F (36.7°C), while in the late afternoons, it might reach slightly above average at 99°F (37.2°C).

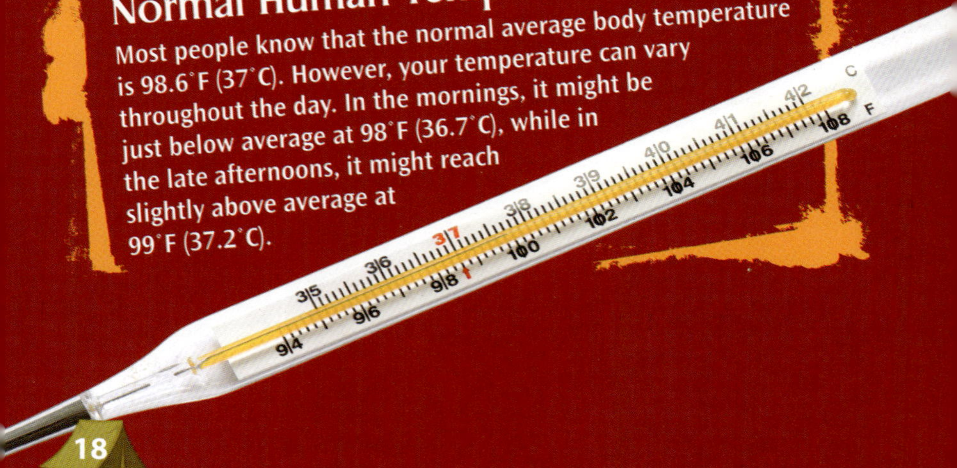

Hyperthermia

On the other end of the scale is **hyperthermia**. As you might guess, it means "overheated." Staying cool and not overheating should be a priority in hot and dry conditions. An easy way to do this is by staying out of direct sunlight and wind. It is best to find calm, cool, shady spots to rest. Keep physical exertion to a minimum. Above all, drink plenty of water.

Thermal imagery captures a hand under normal conditions (left) and a hand exposed to extreme cold temperatures (right).

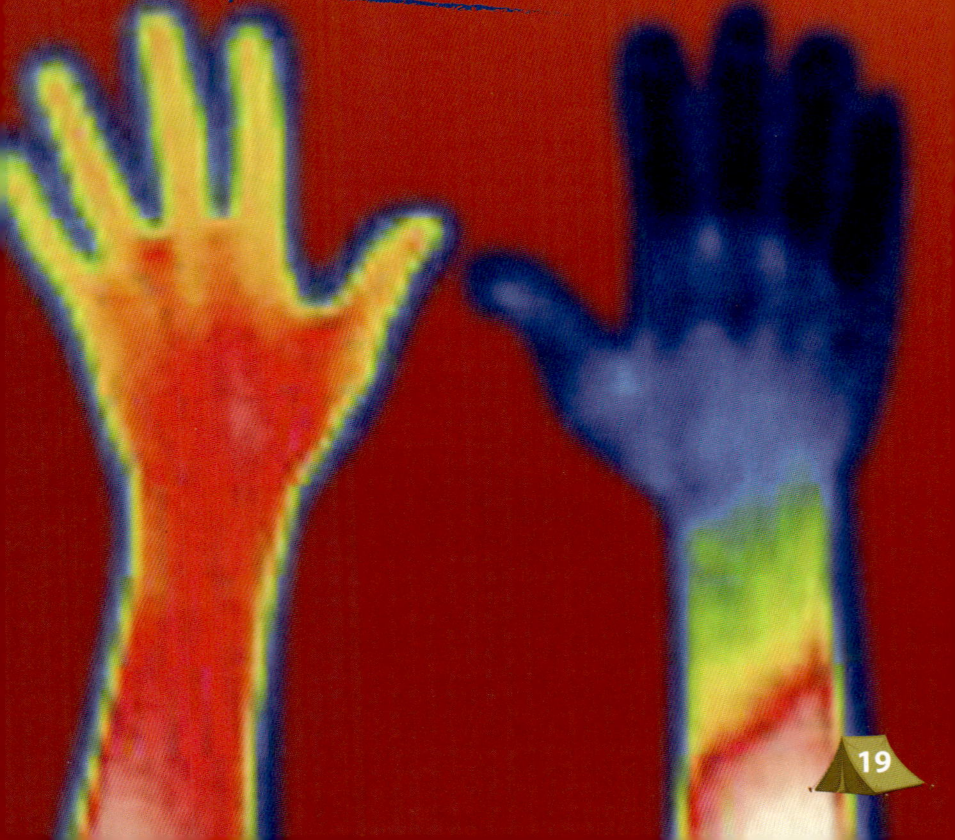

Hypothermia and Hyperthermia

There are many symptoms or signs a person might show if experiencing hypothermia, hyperthermia, or any of the progressive stages. Some of the symptoms to watch for are shown here.

Hypothermia ← colder			Safe Zone
Death Zone (core temp. = 87°F to 90°F = 30.6°C to 32.2°C)	**Advancing Symptoms** (core temp. = 91°F to 94°F = 32.8°C to 34.4°C)	**Early Symptoms** (core temp. = 95°F to 96°F = 35°C to 35.6°C)	**Safe** (core temp. = 98°F to 99°F = 36.7°C to 37.2°C)
waves of shivering inability to walk speech almost impossible to understand	intense shivering stumbling slurred speech no effort to protect self skin appears ashen gray and cold	shivering numbness confusion decreased awareness	optimal core body temperature range

Hyperthermia warmer →		
Heat Cramps (core temp. = 99.1°F to 100°F = 37.3°C to 37.8°C)	**Heat Exhaustion** (core temp. = 101°F to 102°F = 38.3°C to 38.9°C)	**Heat Stroke** (core temp. = 103°F to 106°F = 39.4°C to 41.1°C)
thirst	excessive thirst	rapid, weak pulse
headache	increased headaches and dizziness	enlarged pupils
dizziness	increased sweating	seizures
heavy sweating	overall weakness	delirium and lack of awareness
abdominal spasms	confusion and decreased awareness	loss of consciousness
loss of physical coordination	rapid pulse and shallow, rapid breathing	uneven breathing
	cool, pale, moist skin	hot, flushed, dry skin

Clothes: First Line of Defense

In reality, your first layer of protection from exposure is the clothes you wear. People make clothing choices every day. Some people focus on fashion and style. Most of the time, that works out fine. But there are other times when clothing choices may be the difference between life and death. Don't underestimate the importance of wearing the right clothes for the climate and time of year.

People who live in extreme conditions have learned from experience to be prepared. In areas with harsh winters, smart preparations include thick, warm socks and boots and heavy jackets over multiple layers of clothes. In areas with blazing summers, people know to wear single layers of clothing made of light, **breathable** fabrics. They know, too, to stay out of the sun during the middle of the day.

Covering Up

Covering your skin is essential in cold weather to preserve your body heat. But covering up can be important in heat as well. It can protect the skin from sunburn and also help body sweat do what it is supposed to do: keep the body cool as it evaporates.

Dressing properly in extreme weather conditions is important.

Fabrics

An important consideration in choosing clothes is the fabrics they are made of. There are several different possibilities. Ask yourself: What are your plans for the day? What do you expect the clothes to do for you? Use your answers to help select the right clothes.

There are two main categories when it comes to fabrics: natural and man-made. Natural fabrics include fibers made of wool, cotton, and silk. Man-made fabrics include fibers made of polyester, nylon, and **polypropylene**. Some fabrics may be blends of different materials. Each type has its own characteristics and offers something different to the wearer.

Remember that when it comes to survival, preparation is key. Knowing your fabrics helps you to prepare for the right conditions. Take a look at this chart and what the fabrics do. Then, investigate them yourself. Become your own expert. What works for you?

Get Down!

Down is a natural **insulator** that is basically the feathers of ducks or geese. It is usually packed inside shells of other materials for use as a lightweight insulator.

STOP! THINK...

- What fabric might be good to wear outdoors on a cold, winter's day?
- What fabric might be good to wear on a day hike at a coastal beach?
- Reading this chart, in what ways do you make good fabric and clothing choices on an average day?

Fabric	Source	Positive Property	Negative Property	Best Use
Wool	hair of sheep, goats, alpacas	good insulator; fire resistant; absorbs moisture; retains insulation ability when wet	bulky; some wools are scratchy; comparatively heavy	excellent all-around fabric; great in cold weather
Cotton	cotton plant	comfort and feel; sun protection; absorbs moisture; breathable	holds moisture (deadly in cold); no insulation when wet	heat of summer for wicking moisture and heat
Silk	cocoons of silkworms	very strong fabric; comfortable; lightweight; absorbs moisture	weakens in sunlight; wrinkles easily; expensive	good all-around fabric
Polyester	petroleum polymer	strong fabric; decent insulator; wicks moisture; lightweight	melts when hot	best added to other fabrics to enhance strength
Nylon	petroleum polymer	strong fabric; good for wind and water protection; lightweight	melts when hot; low breathability	external layer for wind and rain protection

Note: Information found in this table is subjective. Opinions and experiences may vary.

Hats Off!

When it comes to protection from the elements, hot or cold, a hat is one of the most important things you can wear. A hat provides protection from both the sun and wind. It can keep your head warm and keep your body's internal heat from escaping through the top of your head.

When it comes to hats, *lightweight* and *breathable* are the important factors for both warm and hot weather. You don't need anything on your head that weighs you down or creates a strain—especially in a survival situation. You want to be able to move easily and see clearly. A hat shouldn't prevent you from doing these things.

For cold weather, you'll want something to keep your head warm. Beanies or knit caps are good headwear for cold conditions. In warm weather, a wide brim to protect your eyes and skin from the sun is important. Straw hats can be especially useful since they are both lightweight and breathable.

In normal conditions, take time to experiment with fabrics to see which feels most comfortable to you and provides either the warmth or shade protection that you need. Then, in a survival situation, you'll have the best hat.

Flap Hat

The French Foreign Legion hat, or flap hat, gives ideal protection in extreme heat and sun. It is made of light-colored and lightweight fabric with a brim over the eyes and a flap protecting the ears and neck. This hat is an excellent choice for extremely hot, bright climates. It is also a good choice for an emergency supply bag.

Be Cool

In extreme heat, soaking a cloth in water and placing it on your head under a hat can be an excellent way to stay cool. A wet rag can also be tied around your neck to help keep the body cool.

Bandanas

Bandanas or kerchiefs are excellent all-around tools for survival and can be used in many different ways. The most obvious ways are the ones we see often: people wearing them as headbands, hats, or around their necks. Worn in these ways, they provide protection from the sun and keep sweat and hair out of the eyes. But they can be used in other ways, too. They can be worn over the nose to protect against smoke, dust, and bugs. They can be used as hot pads, water filters, napkins, first-aid bandages, or slings. Things can be wrapped and carried in bandanas, or several bandanas tied together can make a rope of sorts. You can even blow your nose into one! There's no end to the uses for good bandanas.

It's a good idea to carry a bandana with you at all times. If not at all times, at least carry them when you go camping, hiking, or when you go outdoors for an extended period of time. They are useful under regular circumstances—and they can be essential when it comes to survival.

Keep Them Handy

Day to day, it's easy to keep a bandana handy. Simply tie one onto your school backpack, or keep one in your back pocket.

Signal Flag

Bandanas can be used as a signal flag if you are lost and hoping for rescue. A bright color would be best for signaling, so in general, it's best to carry brightly colored bandanas.

Best Foot Forward!

Protecting the feet is an important part of survival; in fact, it can be critical. Having good, sturdy shoes helps. For outdoor activities, boots or athletic shoes are the most common and sensible choices. However, there are many different kinds of sandals designed for rugged outdoor use as well.

Outdoor footwear should be well constructed and well made. The footwear should have rugged, high-quality, rubber or **composite** soles. Footwear should not be too tight; it should allow room for insulating socks. Too tight or too loose shoes may cause blisters. If you are hiking, leave room in the toes of the shoes so that your toes don't get compressed when walking downhill.

As always, it is best to be prepared, and this also applies when it comes to your footwear. Don't go hiking in flip-flops, and don't go out in the rain in canvas tennis shoes. Ensure that your feet are warm enough in cold weather because your toes are among the first things to freeze in extreme conditions. Be sure, too, that your feet stay dry, as dampness can make them freeze in the cold or develop fungi and other nasty conditions in the heat. Make sure your footwear is always right for the weather, for your activities, and for your feet's best protection.

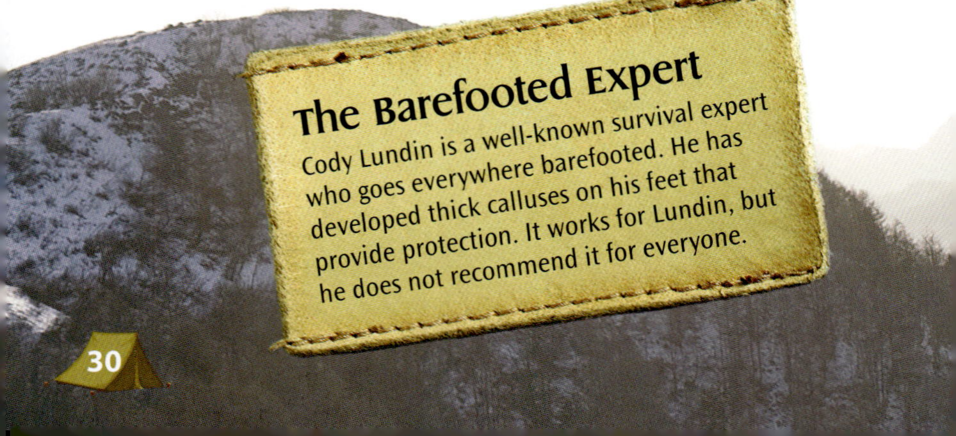

The Barefooted Expert

Cody Lundin is a well-known survival expert who goes everywhere barefooted. He has developed thick calluses on his feet that provide protection. It works for Lundin, but he does not recommend it for everyone.

First Shoes

Indigenous peoples wore sandals made of leather or plant materials. They also had simple boots or moccasins made of leather.

Under Cover

You can think of shelter as an extension of your clothing. In most situations, you will need more than your clothes to protect you. An outer shelter of some kind is necessary, and there are many options.

Imagine you are in a survival situation, perhaps lost in the wilderness. Then, you remember the OODA Loop (observe, orient, decide, act). As part of your decision process, you decide it is best to stay where you are and spend the night rather than hike out after dark. The best and easiest option for you will be finding an existing shelter, such as a small structure with a porch or an extended roof.

Of course, it's not likely that a convenient structure will be suddenly available to you. So, what do you do? You need to improvise and adapt. Consider what materials or equipment you have with you. If you came prepared with a tent, then your problem is solved. Perhaps you have a tarp and some **cordage**. You can set up the tarp by a tree with the cordage to make a **lean-to** or tarp tent. Or, if your car broke down in the middle of nowhere but is otherwise in good condition, it can provide you with necessary shelter.

Home

Besides keeping a person warm and dry, a shelter can also give emotional and mental comfort. Even temporary shelters can do this. Having a base or a home helps provide a person with an **intangible** anchor.

Should You Walk It?

If you are lost or stranded in a survival situation, you have to decide whether to hike or stay put, especially at night. Consider this situation: You are stranded but know that the nearest town is 12 miles away. You can walk 3 miles per hour. It is 2.5 hours until nightfall. How many miles can you walk before dark? What should you do?

The Right Site

In the same survival situation just discussed, maybe none of the mentioned shelters is an option for you. You may just need to use what nature provides.

Survival expert David Holladay developed the Five Ws of site selection, and they are worth remembering. The Five Ws offer guidance and insights for finding the right spot.

David Holladay's Five Ws

- **Widowmakers:** These are dead trees and other precarious structures that may collapse on you. Avoid them.
- **Water:** You want to have shelter near a water source. Don't be too close, as it will likely be colder there than elsewhere, and there are more insects at water's edge. The noise of the running water can also be annoying. At the same time, you don't want to build your shelter in a dry creek bed, which might be exposed to a flash flood.
- **Wigglies:** These are bugs, insects, snakes, and other creepy crawlers. Beware of anthills, snake burrows, and other such animal homes.
- **Wind:** It can dry you out and rob your body of heat, so it's crucial to build your shelter in an area that is naturally protected from wind.
- **Wood:** You need a supply, as it may be important for building a shelter or a fire.

Natural Shelters

With just a little added work, nature may provide a shelter. Low tree branches may be perfectly situated so that all you have to do is place a few more branches against the tree to reinforce the shelter. Rock overhangs with a few well-placed tree branches may also provide good protection.

Don't Let the Bedbugs Bite!

Part of having a shelter includes a place to sleep. If you are building a shelter with natural materials, build your bed first and then create the shelter around it.

You might ask, "A bed? Can't I just sleep on the ground?" Actually, the ground is usually much colder than your body, especially at night. The ground can draw the heat right out of you! You need to insulate your body from the ground. You can do this by building a small platform or pile, using tree branches. It is a good idea to add many layers of leaves, grasses, and other **vegetation** to the bedding as well. Make sure the materials are dry, and the more you put down, the better. Remember, you will be lying on it all night, and it will become quite flattened by morning. In fact, poking small holes throughout the bedding will help provide insulation and prevent **conductive** heat loss.

One important tip: when gathering your bedding materials, check for insects, snakes, and spiders by raking a long stick through the materials. Also, shake the materials as you carry them to your bedding area so all wigglies will fall away.

Poison-Free Bed

When building your bed, be careful not to use poisonous plants such as poison ivy, poison oak, oleander, and so on. You don't need to add to your troubles!

DIG DEEPER!

Build a Lean-To

A lean-to is probably the simplest shelter to make out of natural materials. It is set up so that leaning several poles and branches against a horizontal pole or tree branch creates a roof/wall. Three sides of the lean-to are open, unless additional branches are placed over the ends. Here's how you build a lean-to:

- Make sure your lean-to is oriented so that the wall protects you from wind. To do that, pay attention to which way the wind is blowing.
- Place two vertical poles, called *uprights*, several feet apart.
- Rest a horizontal pole, called a *crossbeam*, across the tops of the two uprights. Sometimes, you may find a low branch on a tree that will work perfectly as a crossbeam where it is, so pay attention to your surroundings.
- Gather several long branches and begin leaning them against the crossbeam. Continue this process until you have a roof/wall several inches thick. It is your protection from the wind and rain.
- Keep an open side to your lean-to so that it is possible to build a fire and stay warm. If your lean-to is enclosed, trapped smoke from the fire cannot escape and can be deadly to you.

Lean-to Calculations

A lean-to needs to be big enough to offer protection for a person lying down. An extra foot on either end should do this. That means the crossbeam should be at least 6 inches longer on each end than the lean-to width so that the beam rests securely atop the uprights. For a 6-foot man, how far apart should the uprights be placed? What should be the minimum length of the crossbeam for this lean-to?

A-Frame Shelter

Another good shelter that can be made from natural materials is an A-frame. It is similar to a lean-to; however, with the A-frame, you lean poles and branches on both sides of the crossbeam in an upside-down V shape. In addition, one end of the crossbeam may lean against the ground, while the other end is supported off the ground by one or two upright poles. You may have less room in an A-frame than in a lean-to, but you will have more protection from a shifting wind.

Keeping Warm

For cooler temperatures, build a shelter with two layers of cover. Stretch flat one large piece of material and attach it to four corner poles. Then, stretch another large piece of material about 12 to 18 inches (30 to 45 centimeters) above the first one. The two layers act as insulation to keep the inside warmer than the outside.

Body Hollow

What if you don't have any supplies and you just need to find some basic protection? You can make a body hollow. To do this, first dig a hole in the ground as long as your body and one to two feet (30 to 60 centimeters) deep. If you don't have a digging tool, you can use a sturdy stick with a sharpened chisel point on one end. Use it to loosen and break up the dirt, which you can then scoop out with your hands. Line the hole with tree branches or other plant material. If available, cover the hole with branches for added protection, keeping one end open. This makes a simple but effective shelter, especially from the wind and cold.

Survival and Self-Reliance

The information in this book covers just a small part of what a person should know about surviving exposure and the shelter needed. You can continue to investigate survival methods and ideas for yourself.

More than anything, remember that you can't control your circumstances. You can't control everything happening around you. But you *can* control your attitude and how you respond to circumstances and events. So, stay positive. Attitude often makes all the difference!

Of course, a person in a tough situation still needs to be realistic and assess the situation honestly. But, to survive, you can't let things get you down. There are *always* possibilities, and you can *always* find a way. Think and plan ahead. Keep your cool.

In the end, you are the most important factor in the survival equation! Keep thinking, and keep a good attitude. You've got what it takes to survive!

Keep Thinking!

There are hundreds of books, old and new, on the topic of survival. There are many classes available, too. But be careful where you get your information! Many people have good intentions but may be badly misinformed about survival. It is best to approach information critically.

A True-Life Survival Story

Thirteen-year-old Charlie Finlayson was hiking with his father, David, when a boulder fell and struck David, who was severely injured. Charlie cared for his father until David urged him to go for help. Charlie was reluctant but followed his father's advice: "Stay calm." After hiking a few miles, Charlie found other hikers who helped him. Fortunately, everything worked out for Charlie and his father.

Glossary

breathable—having a loose enough weave of threads and fabric makeup so that air circulates easily through it

catastrophic—disastrous

competent—able to

composite—made up of different materials

composure—calmness of mind

conductive—transmitting through touch

cordage—ropes or cords

creature comforts—luxuries; things to make life easier

dire—horrible; disastrous

elements—weather conditions

exposure—the act of being open to extreme weather conditions for a dangerous amount of time,

hydration—the condition of having a sufficient supply of liquid, especially water

hyperthermia—the condition in which the temperature of the body is very high

hypothermia—the condition in which the temperature of the body is very low

industrialized—consisting of many industries and businesses

insulator—a fabric that helps keep a person warm

intangible—not able to be held or felt

lean-to—temporary shelter made by leaning branches or other materials against a fixed object

natural disaster—destructive and devastating occurrence that originates from a natural event, usually weather related (for example, a hurricane) or a natural earth process (for example, an earthquake)

navigation—the process of finding the way from one place to another

orienteering—a group of activities that uses navigation skills to get from one place to another

polypropylene—various thermoplastic materials used to make fabrics

priorities—things that deserve attention before others

resources—basic supplies

sanitation—the process of keeping areas clean

survival skills—abilities to provide for the basic needs of life

vegetation—plant life

wicking—causing moisture to be pulled away from the surface

Index

Check It Out!

Books

George, Jean Craighead. 2004. *My Side of the Mountain*. Puffin Books.

Lundin, Cody. 2003. *98.6 Degrees*. Gibbs Smith.

_____. 2007. *When All Hell Breaks Loose*. Gibbs Smith.

Nyerges, Christopher. 2014. *How to Survive Anywhere: A Guide for Urban, Suburban, Rural, and Wilderness Environments*. Stackpole Books.

O'Dell, Scott. 2010. *Island of the Blue Dolphins*. HMH Books for Young Readers.

Olsen, Larry Dean. 1990. *Outdoor Survival Skills*. Chicago Review Press.

Paulsen, Gary. 2006. *Hatchet*. Simon & Schuster Books for Young Readers.

Rice, William B. 2013. *Survival! Desert*. Teacher Created Materials.

_____. 2013. *Survival! Jungle*. Teacher Created Materials.

_____. 2013. *Survival! Ocean*. Teacher Created Materials.

Websites

Lundin, Cody. *Aboriginal Living Skills School*. http://www.codylundin.com/.

Noble, Christian. *Master Woodsman*. http://masterwoodsman.com/.

Nyerges, Christopher. *School of Self-Reliance*. http://www.christophernyerges.com/.

Magazines/Journals

Richie, Charlie (ed.). *Backwoodsman*. Backwoodsman Magazine.

Society of Primitive Technology. *Bulletin of Primitive Technology*. Society of Primitive Technology, 2014.

Try It!

The snow is falling, and it doesn't look like it's going to stop any time soon. You've decided to stop traveling for the night and need to build a shelter. Draw a picture or construct a model of the shelter that you would build. Be sure to include the following:

- What are the measurements for how big your actual shelter would be?
- List the materials you would need to use.
- Describe why you would choose this type of shelter.
- What would you build to sleep on?
- What are your fire placement plans?

About the Author

William B. Rice is a native Californian who enjoys the fundamental skills involved in survival and the simple and traditional ways of life. Bill is a geologist who works for the state of California to protect water quality. He is passionate about the well-being of planet Earth. Bill has authored many books for children on science topics, especially those concerned with the environment and protecting it. He enjoys spending time outdoors and is an avid camper, hiker, and naturalist. He lives in the Inland Empire with his wife and sons.

Answers

page 7—78°F

page 13—The fabric can be used to help shelter the group collectively, or it can be cut into four equal pieces. The benefit of equal squares, triangles, or strips should be considered.

page 17—3.2 hours

page 33—You can only walk about 7.5 miles, so it's probably best to stay the night and walk in the morning.

page 39—The uprights should be set 8 feet apart. The crossbeam should be at least 9 feet long.